NEW ZEALAND'S

NORTH ISLAND

FROM ABOVE

DAVID WALL

Text by Alison Dench

First published in 2007 by New Holland Publishers (NZ) Ltd
Auckland • Sydney • London • Cape Town

www.newhollandpublishers.co.nz

ISBN: 978 1 86966 174 8

Design: Dexter Fry

A catalogue record for this book is available from the
    National Library of New Zealand

10 9 8 7 6 5 4 3 2 1

Colour reproduction by S C (Sang Choy) International
    Pte Ltd, Singapore
Printed by Times Offset (M) Sdn Bhd, Malaysia.

Front cover: Cape Maria van Diemen, Northland.
Back cover: Oriental Bay, Wellington; Chateau hotel and
    Mt Ngauruhoe, central North Island.
Page 2: Cook's Cove, Motuarohia (Roberton Island), Bay of
    Islands, Northland.

Also from David Wall and New Holland:

New Zealand's South Island from Above
ISBN: 978 1 86966 175 5

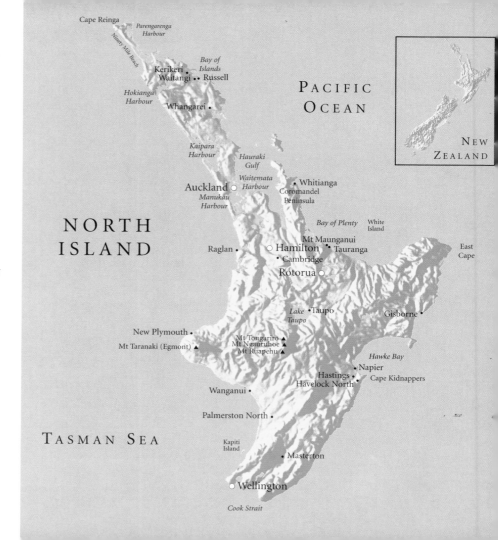

INTRODUCTION

FROM ANY ANGLE or elevation the North Island of New Zealand is spectacularly beautiful and varied. But from the air, its rumbling volcanoes, sweeping shores and branching sandy bays, green rolling hills and dense rainforests, its tranquil lakes and buzzing urban centres, seem to take on a new form. Looking down, it is easy to see the true shape of the land – and the way people occupy it.

The aerial view reveals every fold and fault of the landscape, every scarp and rift. This island is geologically young and is still maturing – volcanic lava and ash have time and again broken through the earth's crust and covered much of the island, shaping hills and valleys and creating mountains that rise dramatically from the plains. And that remoulding continues today, with active volcanic zones and fault lines extending down from the Bay of Plenty to Wellington.

A bird's-eye perspective also highlights the vivid contrasts at the margins of the land. On the east coast people have made their mark everywhere. The complex bays and sheltered inlets have long been havens for settlement, and the benign beaches are now also a playground for holidaymakers. On the western shore, where the sea is met by high cliffs and hard rock and the coastline is stark and simple, the traces of people are few and far between.

The North Island, youthful and vibrant, is astonishingly diverse in landscape, climate and population. The view from above allows a unique perspective and a unique insight.

DUNEDIN-BASED DAVID WALL developed an interest in photography during travels overseas. These included several years' work as an expedition tour leader in Africa, which resulted in the publication of his first book, *Visions of Africa*, in 1998. Since then David has built up a New Zealand photographic library offering more than 100,000 images covering the country, both at ground level and from a variety of aircraft. He has also been creating an online collection of Australian images. David has published many pictorial books with New Holland, including *This is New Zealand*, *New Zealand in Colour*, *New Zealand Through the Seasons* and *New Zealand from Above*.

LEFT Remote Cape Reinga, where the Tasman Sea and Pacific Ocean meet, is of special significance to Maori as the place the spirits of the dead leave the mainland on their journey to the spiritual homeland of Hawaiki.

ABOVE Ninety Mile Beach sweeps down the western coast of the Aupouri Peninsula. The golden sands serve multiple purposes, as swimming beach, surf-casting spot – and public road.

LEFT   The white sands of Parengarenga Harbour, close to the northern tip of New Zealand, are among the purest in New Zealand. The harbour's wetlands are an important staging post for migratory shore birds, supporting up to 20,000 birds at a time.

ABOVE Kerikeri Inlet in the Bay of Islands became one of the earliest sites of European settlement in 1819. The Stone Store (1836) and the neighbouring Mission House (1822) are architectural treasures, among the oldest buildings in New Zealand.

RIGHT In subtropical Kerikeri, market gardeners grow vegetables, and windbreaks protect groves of citrus fruits, macadamia nuts, kiwifruit and tamarillo. In recent years vines for wine making have steadily been taking the place of the orchards.

ABOVE An imposing naval flagstaff marks the place New Zealand's founding document, the Treaty of Waitangi, was signed by representatives of the British Crown and Maori leaders. The ceremony took place in the grounds of the home of the first British Resident, James Busby.

RIGHT In the early days of European settlement the quiet historic town of Russell was much rowdier, nicknamed the 'hellhole of the Pacific'. Above the bay is Maiki Hill, where Hone Heke cut down the flagstaff four times, starting a nine-month war with the British in 1845.

LEFT   The Bay of Islands is a favourite place for game fishing, diving and sailing. Motuarohia Island, actually two islands joined together by a sandy tombolo, is just one of the many islands, large and small, you can visit.

ABOVE   Motukokako (Piercy Island) rises 152 metres above the Pacific Ocean off Cape Brett. Its famous 'hole in the rock', scoured by wind and waves, is visited daily by passenger cruises from Paihia.

TOP RIGHT Maori visitors to Waiwera, just north of Auckland, have for centuries immersed themselves in the warm therapeutic mineral waters. Waiwera has the oldest spa in New Zealand, opened in 1875, and its 1500-metre aquifer is the source for bottled mineral water.

BELOW RIGHT At Gulf Harbour, on the Whangaparaoa Peninsula north of Auckland, boaties can tie up right next to their own homes. The recent housing development also boasts a world-class golf course.

FAR RIGHT North Head, in the plush Auckland suburb of Devonport, offers a commanding view of the entrance to the Waitemata Harbour. The volcanic cone is riddled with tunnels, bunkers and gun emplacements left over from World War II.

LEFT The Auckland harbour bridge, opened in 1959, links the North Shore with the central business district, saving more than 40 kilometres of road travel. Nearby the sheltered waters of the Waitemata offer safe moorings for yachts.

ABOVE Auckland's downtown wharf area bustles with activity. Visiting cruise liners and superyachts dock at Princes Wharf at the bottom of the city's main street, while older vessels are on display at the maritime museum next door.

RIGHT The tall office buildings of Queen Street are a symbol of Auckland's position as the country's financial powerhouse. The Sky Tower, the tallest freestanding structure in the southern hemisphere, rises above them all.

FAR RIGHT One Tree Hill, or Maungakiekie, is at the heart of Auckland's largest city park. Once an impressive Maori fortress supporting 5000 people, it is now an expanse of green pasture grazed by sheep and cattle, along with areas of parkland and gardens.

FAR LEFT Amid the leafy parkland of the Auckland Domain, the Winter Garden is a year-round attraction. Built after World War I and refurbished in 2006, it is home to a fernery and two glasshouses: one for temperate plants, the other tropical. The nearby War Memorial Museum houses priceless collections of Maori and Pacific treasures and artefacts from the nation's wider social and scientific history.

LEFT Musick Point reaches from Howick into the Waitemata Harbour, which made it an excellent site for a radio contact station for shipping and aircraft in World War II. The Howick Golf Club makes the most of the spectacular sea views.

LEFT Waiheke Island, once a holiday destination, is now within commuting distance of Auckland, seen here as a hazy sprawl beyond the shield volcano Rangitoto. The island's many bays and inlets are havens for boats cruising the Hauraki Gulf, while its sunny slopes produce superb red-wine grapes.

ABOVE Tiritiri Matangi, north of Auckland, is an island sanctuary. More than a quarter of a million native trees have been planted and mammalian predators have been eradicated, making it safe to release such threatened and endangered birds as little spotted kiwi and takahe.

RIGHT   The wild coast at Piha has an irresistible allure for surfers, swimmers, fishers and walkers. Only 45 minutes from the city, the west coast and the forested Waitakere Ranges behind are a magnet for Aucklanders at weekends.

FAR RIGHT   A sandy bar makes navigating the narrow entrance to the Manukau Harbour south-west of Auckland a difficult task. In New Zealand's worst shipwreck, the bar claimed HMS *Orpheus* in 1863, with the loss of 189 lives.

LEFT   The pinkish sands of Cathedral Cove, on the Coromandel's Pacific coast, are accessible only by boat or on foot. A huge rock arch cuts through the pohutukawa-dotted headland to Mares Leg Cove beyond.

ABOVE   There's space for everyone on Hot Water Beach, south of Whitianga, where in summer lifeguards keep an eye on swimmers braving the powerful surf. At low tide it's possible to dig your own pool in the sand and soak in thermal mineral water.

ABOVE   Hahei is a flourishing holiday town. The clean clear water and the sheltered sandy beach provide plenty of activities for vacationing families – swimming, sailing, fishing, kayaking and diving.

RIGHT   The purpose-built resort town of Pauanui, with its Waterways development, was a forested sand spit only 40 years ago. The Coromandel settlement has a small permanent population but explodes into life over the summer holiday period.

FAR RIGHT   Whitianga is home to a fleet of commercial fishing boats, charter vessels and private yachts and launches. A passenger ferry plies the short stretch of fast-moving water between the town and the Cooks Beach area on the other side of the harbour.

FAR LEFT The relaxed, arty beach town of Raglan sits at the mouth of a large harbour that is perfect for swimming, kayaking and windsurfing – at the right tide. Its ocean beaches are famed for their surf breaks.

TOP LEFT The Waikato River winds through Hamilton on its way from Lake Taupo to the sea south of Auckland. Hamilton is the largest inland city in New Zealand, having progressed far beyond its original role as a provincial farming service town.

BELOW LEFT Almost every spare square metre of land in the Waikato is devoted to farming. Fertile soils, good sunshine and regular rainfall make the plains and gently rolling hills perfect pastures for dairy cows.

LEFT The volcanic cone of Mount Maunganui stands guard over the southern entrance to the Tauranga Harbour. Known to Maori as Mauao, and held sacred by them, the mountain was the site of an immense – and much fought-over – pa that was finally abandoned in 1820.

ABOVE The main drawcards of the resort town of Mt Maunganui, between the Pacific Ocean and Tauranga Harbour, are its magnificent white-sand beach, sunny weather and reliable surf. In the summer holidays, and especially around New Year, the settlement has a carnival atmosphere.

LEFT Seething, simmering White Island, 50 kilometres off the Bay of Plenty coast, is New Zealand's most active volcano. Its Maori name, Whakaari, means 'to expose to view' and the island can indeed be seen from almost everywhere on the Bay shore.

ABOVE At the Champagne Pool near Rotorua, boiling, fizzing water rich with minerals breaks through the earth's crust and produces the striking colours. Geothermal wonders – bubbling mud, geysers and therapeutic mineral springs – have brought tourists to the area for well over a century.

RIGHT Lake Tarawera, surrounded by bush and with its own settlement, is one of 11 fishable lakes in the Rotorua district. There are 16 lakes in all, and they are also used for swimming, waterskiing, kayaking and boating.

FAR RIGHT Mokoia Island in Lake Rotorua has a special place in Maori tradition as the home of Tutanekai, whose lover Hinemoa was so devoted she swam across the lake to be with him. Rotorua is today an important centre for Maori culture.

ABOVE   The Taupo area is a thrilling playground for the adventurous. Jet boats, which are a New Zealand invention, can race up shallow rivers at speed, handle churning rapids and turn on a sixpence.

RIGHT   At Huka Falls, near Taupo, the Waikato River is forced through a narrow rock canyon and then thunders 11 metres down into a circular pool. Appropriately enough, the Maori name Huka means 'foam'.

ABOVE Little Lake Rotongaio abuts New Zealand's largest lake, Taupo. There is excellent boat fishing for trout, while the streams that feed the great lake are legendary for fly fishing.

LEFT Taupo sits at the edge of the lake that shares its name, beside the Waikato River and in the shadow of Tauhara. The main town of the Central Plateau, Taupo is known for watersports, fishing and adventure tourism.

LEFT When it opened in 1970, the perfectly manicured Wairakei International Golf Course near Taupo was New Zealand's first world-class championship course. There is no club here; instead the course relies on greens fees paid by players from around the country and overseas.

ABOVE At the Craters of the Moon thermal area, steam and foul-smelling volcanic gases from subterranean boiling water escape through a thin part of the earth's crust. Taupo is in the very active volcanic zone that stretches from Ruapehu to White Island.

LEFT Few hotels could claim a grander location than that held by the Chateau, nestling close to Mt Ngauruhoe in Tongariro National Park. New Zealand's first national park was gifted to the nation by the Tuwharetoa people to allow the protection of its sacred mountains.

ABOVE Ngauruhoe's symmetrical cone is the result of regular volcanic activity, including more than 70 ash eruptions between 1839 and 1975. According to Maori legend, the distant peak of Taranaki fled to the coast after a feud with his fellow volcanoes.

LEFT The wide open spaces of the Whakapapa Ski Area attract snowsports devotees from all over the North Island and beyond. The ski field, sheltered by the impressive jagged Pinnacles, looks out from Ruapehu to the mountains Ngauruhoe and Tongariro.

ABOVE Ruapehu is the largest of the three volcanoes of Tongariro National Park. On the summit plateau its crater lake is ever-changing, rising and falling, steaming and changing colour, and from time to time spilling out and rushing down the mountainside as a lahar.

RIGHT   After a devastating earthquake in 1931, the Hawke's Bay town of Napier was rebuilt in the style of the time to become the Art Deco capital of the world. Marine Parade, which runs between the city and its shingle beach, is home to the Pania of the Reef statue, the soundshell and sunken gardens.

LEFT   Te Mata Estate is one of the oldest and most respected of Hawke's Bay's many wineries. Thanks to a dry climate and clement growing conditions, the region produces red wines, particularly Cabernet Sauvignon, of very high quality.

ABOVE   The Tukituki River flows from the Ruahine Range to the Pacific Ocean, passing close to Havelock North through fertile river flats below Te Mata Peak. The trout fishing in the river is excellent.

LEFT In spring and summer the sandstone promontory of Cape Kidnappers and rocky Black Reef, at the southern end of Hawke Bay, are a breeding ground for thousands of Australasian gannets.

ABOVE Cape Kidnappers is the world's largest and most accessible mainland gannet colony. Although there is no road nearby, it is possible to walk there along the beach from Clifton – or ride on a tractor trailer.

RIGHT   On a clear day, Taranaki/
Mt Egmont is a presence all over the
Taranaki region. The farming and
beach community of Urenui is some
45 kilometres away, but the peak still
dominates the skyline.

FAR RIGHT   Taranaki/Mt Egmont
rises 2518 metres into the alpine air
above the dense subtropical forests of
Egmont National Park. The volcano last
erupted in about 1755, and part of the
summit collapsed some time in the late
19th century.

LEFT On Kapiti Island near Wellington, native plants and animals are protected and human influences minimised. Visitors to this island sanctuary have a rare chance to see such birds as saddlebacks, kokako, takahe and little spotted kiwi.

ABOVE Titahi Bay, a suburb of Porirua north of Wellington, sits on a peninsula between Cook Strait and Porirua Harbour. The surf off the curving golden-sand beach is among the best in the region.

ABOVE The warped, faulted and folded hills above Plimmerton, near Wellington, are the result of a violent geological past. The area is still tectonically active; the last earthquake to significantly affect the landscape was as recent as 1855.

LEFT Oriental Bay is sandwiched on a thin strip of land between Mt Victoria and Lambton Harbour. With its beach promenade, boat harbour and sandy swimming beach, it is one of Wellington's more desirable addresses.

ABOVE Island Bay, once a seaside resort and now a suburb of Wellington, is sheltered by Taputeranga Island which creates a good anchorage for fishing vessels. In the early 20th century fishermen from the Shetland Islands and Italy settled here.

RIGHT   There are always people around on the Wellington waterfront, playing in Frank Kitts Park, paddling in the harbour, skateboarding, cycling, skating, running, fishing, enjoying the public sculptures or simply sitting in the sun eating a sandwich.

FAR RIGHT   Wellington's business district is built on one of the city's few tracts of flat land, although much of that land had to be reclaimed from the harbour. Reclamation work began in the mid-19th century and continued intermittently until the 1970s.

FAR LEFT The Beehive has become an icon of the nation's capital, Wellington. The unique circular building opened in 1981 to house the offices of government ministers but its many wedge-shaped rooms turned out to be impractical.

LEFT Wellington's stadium has been nicknamed the Cake Tin. During autumn and winter the stadium regularly echoes with the roar of the capital's famously enthusiastic rugby fans. It is also a venue for football, cricket and rock concerts.

FOLLOWING PAGE The North and South Islands are linked by a regular vehicle ferry service between Wellington and Picton. Big vessels like the *Aratere* make light work of Cook Strait's sometimes rough seas.